LOVE
GIRLS! GIRLS! GIRLS!
I ROCK
D1224396

First published in 2009 by Parragon

1 3 5 7 9 10 8 6 4 2

Printed and bound in China

CONTENTS

GIRLS ROCK!

STAR GIRL

STAR GIRL

DISNEY DIVA!

Like *Hannah Montana*? We betcha love Selena Gomez too, Disney's brightest new talent. She sings, she acts and she's already a style icon—we heart Selena!

PSSSt!

Selena's celeb crushes are Shia LaBeouf and Emile Hirsch.

PSSSt!

Her fave school subject is Science.

SELENA'S STORY

2002–2005:
Selena's first ever TV role was playing a character called Gianna in the pre-school show *Barney & Friends.*

2006:
At 12, Selena was discovered by Disney in a nationwide talent search and went on to have a guest spot in season two of *The Suite Life of Zac & Cody!*

2007:
Selena appeared in season two of *Hannah Montana* as Mikayla, Hannah's pop rival. Two of our top talents in one show—what more could we wish for?

2008 :
Selena stars as Alex Russo in Disney's *Wizards of Waverly Place.* She even sings the theme tune!

2009-future:
The sky's the limit for this super-talented superstar!

Selena beat stiff competition—including cool Zoey 101 star Alexa Nikolas—to land her role in Wizards of Waverly Place.

ALL ABOUT ASHLEY

HIGH SCHOOL MUSICAL'S FABULOUS MS TISDALE SPILLS ALL ON RUMORS, CELEB PALS AND SHOPPING!

ASHLEY ON...

Life since HSM
"My life has definitely been a lot crazier. I've had a lot of opportunities obviously, but I'm a lot busier."

Strange rumors
"One paper said I changed my outfits five times in a day and called it a five-outfit frenzy. I did change, but it was just because I was doing different talk shows!"

Her look
"I can go from vintage-looking one day to very chic the next. I'm always changing it up."

Celeb pals
"A lot of the celebrities who are my age live like two blocks from each other in LA! So yes, I hang out all the time with Vanessa, Zac, Miley Cyrus and the Jonas Brothers."

TIME OUT WITH TISDALE...

So Ashley, what's your...

Most treasured possession
"A charm bracelet from my grandma."

Best celeb perk
"Free clothes!"

First job
"In a store at the mall."

Fave celeb
"Jessica Simpson—I love her style!"

Secret talent
"Twisting my double-jointed fingers."

Fave animal
"Penguins."

Nickname
"Pookernut!"

MILEY MANIA!

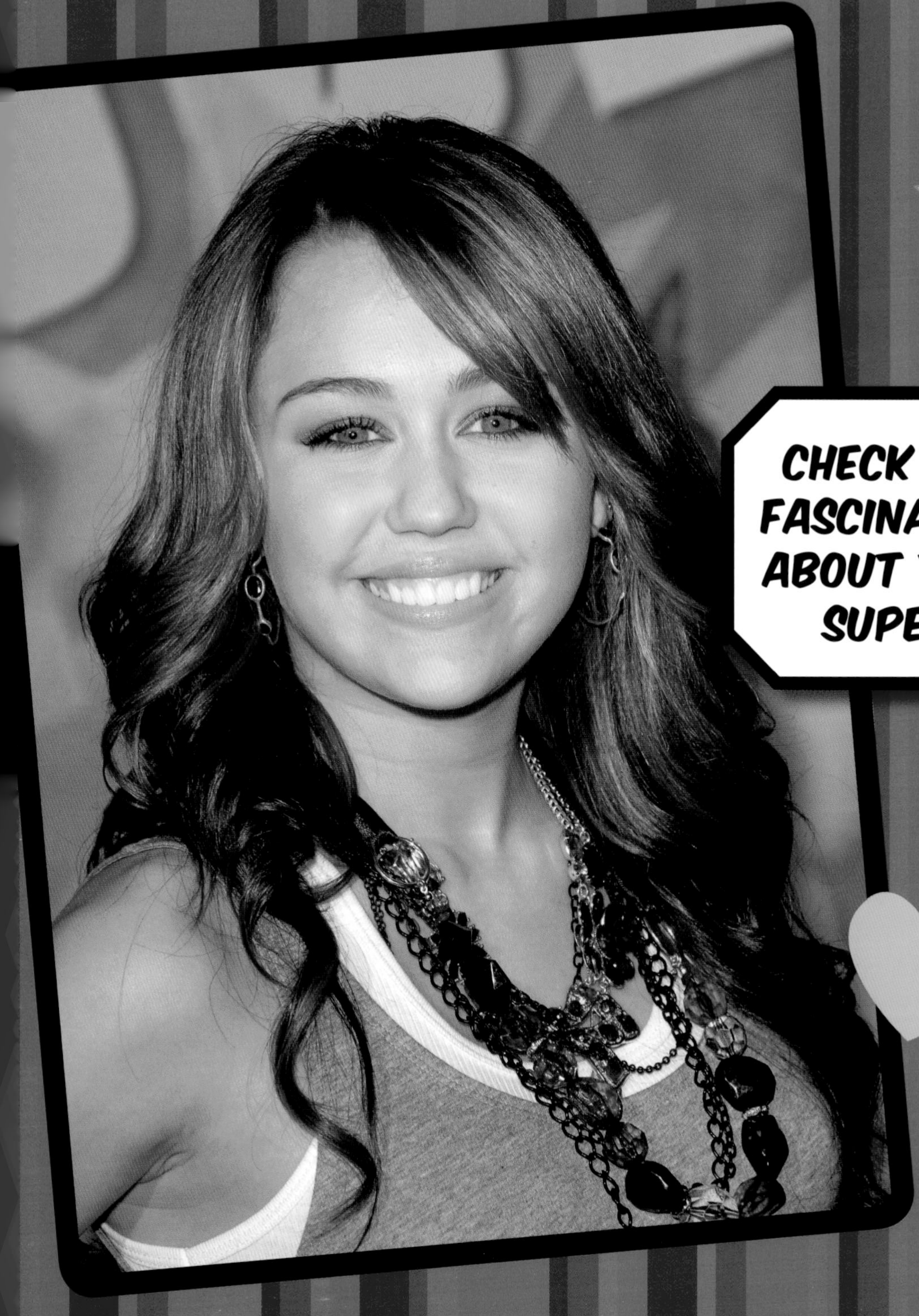

CHECK OUT THESE FASCINATING FACTS ABOUT THE SINGING SUPERSTAR...

Her favorite song to perform live is *See You Again.*

The wig she wears as Hannah is custom-made for her. She takes two on tour and has two back in LA!

Miley doesn't go to school. Instead, she studies on set or on tour for three hours in the mornings.

She's addicted to ketchup and it's her fave thing in the whole world. She even admits to drinking it from the bottle!

She has a diary but, instead of writing her thoughts down, she usually writes songs!

MILEY ON...

The downsides of fame:
"The pressure is definitely hard, but if you know who you are, you'll be fine for the rest of the way."

Being Hannah Montana:
"It's like a dream come true. I get to do everything I love; I've got the best job in the world."

Her dad:
"He loves to embarrass me by yelling things, like 'remember when you were a kid...?' but it's funny. It breaks the ice on photo shoots and on set, so I take it!"

DEMI ROCKS!

She sings, she dances and now she's found mega stardom as the lead in Disney's Camp Rock. This means she got to hang out with the super-cute Jonas Brothers! Could we be more jealous of Demi Lovato?

★ PSSSt! ★

Demi landed her big break in the kids' show Barney & Friends. And that's where she met her BFF, Wizards of Waverly Place star Selena Gomez!

THE WORLD ACCORDING TO DEMI...

Rock what you've got...

"Everyone gets a little self-conscious when they look in the mirror but I don't ever pin-point anything that I don't like about myself. My best feature would have to be my waist. I'm not a toothpick-skinny type. I've got curves and I accentuate them with belts."

Dealing with haters...

"I went through so much rejection from girls at school that I couldn't do acting anymore. But then I started missing it and I decided not to let them stop me following my dream, so I got back into it. That's when things started to roll. Looking back, those girls were giving me a hard time because they were jealous."

The Jonas Brothers are awesome...

"I auditioned for Disney several times and was asked to try out for Camp Rock. But I didn't know the Jonas Brothers were going to be in it before I got the part. They're my role models. Rarely do you run across teenage boys, and ones who are rock stars for that matter, who are as genuine as they are."

Future plans...

"The only thing I see myself doing is music—songwriting or producing. I've never imagined myself in any other business and I've been working in this one since I was five years old! There are other things I could do, but I wouldn't want to!"

AMAZING ABIGAIL

CRYING ON CUE IS ALL IN A DAYS WORK FOR OSCAR-NOMINATED ABIGAIL BRESLIN. BUT SHE STILL HAS TO FIND TIME TO CLEAN HER ROOM!

ABIGAIL'S FAVE...

Disney flick: *Finding Nemo*
Book: *Anne of Green Gables*
Food: Cheesecake, pizza, chili-cheese fries, raspberry mousse, cupcakes
Actresses: Meryl Streep, Judy Garland
Thing to do: Talk and text on her phone!

Abigail is really afraid of heights.

FUN FACTS!

If Abigail wasn't a movie star, she'd like to become a fashion designer or a vet.

Before filming *Nim's Island*, she'd never swam in the sea!

Just because she's a superstar, doesn't mean she escapes her chores—her mom makes her clean her room every week!

If she were a superhero, she'd like to be able to fly and speak every different language.

ALL ABOUT VANESSA

VANESSA HUDGENS IS A CHART-TOPPING SUPERSTAR AND A BIG-SCREEN SUCCESS. SHE'S ALSO DATING THE CUTEST GUY IN CUTESVILLE, ZAC EFRON—WHAT'S HER SECRET?

PSSSt!

If Vanessa could have appeared in any other teen flick it would have been Mean Girls!

Vanessa loves to glam up for the red carpet but when she's off-duty from celebville, her favorite thing to do is pull her hair back in a ponytail, put on a pair of big shades and go see the sights of a new city!

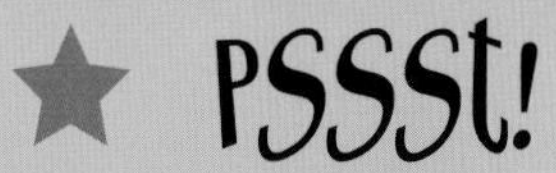

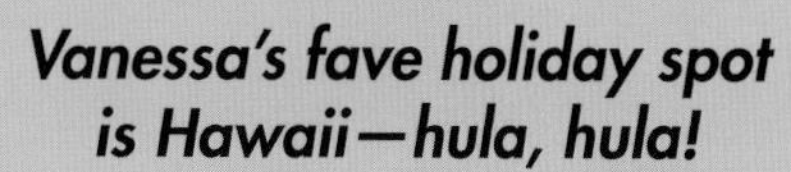

The paparazzi
"It's still weird to me to think people would take pictures of you as you're eating or doing something random."

Publicity
"I love my fans and I want to let them into my world a little bit, but I really am a private person, and I love keeping my life to myself—that's how I've always been."

Being a role model
"I love being a role model because, in Hollywood, there aren't a lot of role models to look up to. The fact that there's now a whole bunch of kids stepping into the limelight, I'm very proud of that."

Family
"I take my family everywhere, especially when I'm touring. It's very hectic and I just couldn't do it without them. I love having them around me."

Her HSM character, Gabriella
"It's been fun watching her grow. She's made hard decisions and become a strong woman. That's the one thing I'm proud of, and I love what she's turned into."

The future
"I'd like to do something totally different. I don't want to go off and shock everybody, but I don't want to keep playing the same role either. I'd like a challenge."

GIRLS ROCK!

You ROCK!

GIRL
WORLD

MAKE YOUR DREAMS COME TRUE

IF YOU WANNA BE THE NEXT MILEY OR RHIANNA, SUCCESS TAKES HARD WORK AND DETERMINATION. HERE'S HOW SOME OF OUR FAVE CELEB-GIRLS REACHED THE TOP OF THEIR GAME...

TOTALLY COOL!

"I've made wrong career choices 'cause I had nothing else to do at the time. You need to follow your head, heart and gut feelings."

Vanessa Hudgens

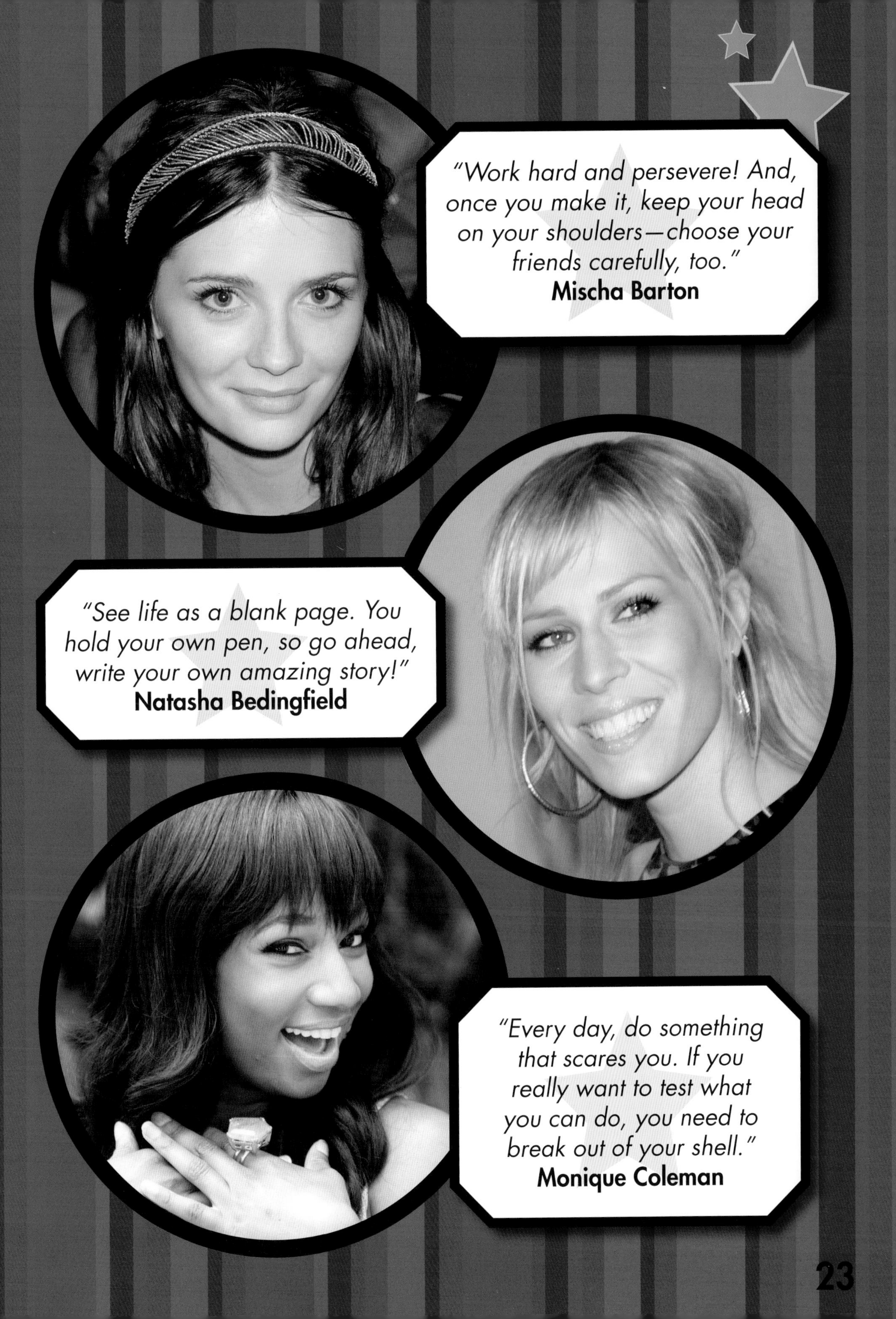
"Work hard and persevere! And, once you make it, keep your head on your shoulders—choose your friends carefully, too."
Mischa Barton
"See life as a blank page. You hold your own pen, so go ahead, write your own amazing story!"
Natasha Bedingfield
"Every day, do something that scares you. If you really want to test what you can do, you need to break out of your shell."
Monique Coleman

BLONDE AMBITION

FIND THE FAIR-HAIRED CELEB GALS HIDDEN IN THE PUZZLE!

Ashley ★ Blake ★ Hayden

Jessica ★ Li-lo ★ Mary-Kate

Avril ★ Gwen

N	Y	G	D	N	J	D	M	D	Q
W	E	K	W	S	F	A	J	E	T
A	L	D	M	I	R	F	K	K	L
V	H	V	Y	Y	L	A	S	B	N
R	S	R	K	A	L	I	L	O	P
I	A	A	L	B	H	Q	E	N	J
L	T	E	R	Y	J	D	S	O	R
E	A	C	I	S	S	E	J	Q	E
B	U	G	W	E	N	Q	I	T	Y
A	S	I	B	J	E	W	X	A	M

FAME GAME

HOW DID OUR FAVORITE CELEB-GIRLS MAKE IT BIG?

BLAKE LIVELY

Blake comes from a family of entertainers—both her parents were actors and all four siblings are in showbiz, too. She got her first role in the movie *Sandman*, as a tooth fairy, and then got her big break with the role of Bridget in *The Sisterhood of the Travelling Pants*. This led to the *Teen Choice Awards*, more movie parts and a juicy role as Serena in *Gossip Girl!*

HAYDEN PANETTIERE

Hayden began modeling at just 11 months old! Her first TV appearance was in a commercial for toys, which led to roles in Soap Operas like *One Life to Live* and *The Guiding Light*. She was still young when she voiced the ant, Dot, in *A Bug's Life* and played *Ally McBeal's* daughter in the hit drama. Now we all know her as the cheerleader in *Heroes* and a campaigner for conservation. She's about to launch a career in music too!

RIHANNA

Born in Barbados, Rihanna was musical from a young age, forming singing groups and performing at high school shows. Her big break came when she was introduced to a record producer vacationing in Barbados. He loved her so much he sent her songs to record companies. One of those demos fell into the hands of Jay-Z, who signed her to his then label, *Def Jam!*

ANNE HATHAWAY

After starting out in high school plays, Anne joined a theater group. Her breakthrough role was in the TV show *Get Real*, which she starred in 'til the series got cancelled. Then she auditioned for the part of Mia in *The Princess Diaries* and won the director over when she fell off her chair! From that, she scored roles in *Ella Enchanted*, *Brokeback Mountain* and fashion fest *The Devil Wears Prada*.

RAVEN SYMONE

Talented Raven began acting as a little girl, starring in commercials from the age of two! Recommended for a role in comedy series *The Cosby Show* by producers, she won the part of cute-as-a-button Olivia Kendall. That led to work in the TV show *Hangin' with Mr Cooper* and the Eddie Murphy movie *Doctor Dolittle*. But it was her own show, *That's So Raven*, which really shot her to superstardom!

ROCK TO THE TOP!

You CAN do it!

Be optimistic. If you don't believe in yourself nobody else will, either. Practice your singing and instrument playing regularly and you'll get there.

Rock it!

If you don't enjoy performing, people won't enjoy your performances. Top stars have electrifying stage presence, so don't just stand there…rock out and raise the roof!

Be yourself!

Copying other artists will only get you so far—to make it big, you need to be original and unique. If you develop your own style in singing, songwriting and stage presence, you'll stand a much better chance of rocking your way to the top.

Keep it real!

The rock-star life isn't all concerts and partying—it can be tough, especially if you're away from home. If you achieve stardom, remember to surround yourself with close friends and family who will always be there for you and help to keep your feet on the ground.

GIRL WORLD

EMMA'S FRIENDSHIP FIXES

IN THE MOVIE *WILD CHILD* 17-YEAR-OLD LA NATIVE, EMMA ROBERTS, PLAYS POPPY. A SPOILED MALIBU PRINCESS, POPPY GETS SHIPPED TO AN ENGLISH BOARDING SCHOOL TO BE STRAIGHTENED OUT. SHE REALIZES EVERY GIRL NEEDS BFFS, EVEN IF SHE DOESN'T KNOW IT. HERE'S EMMA'S GUIDE TO FRIENDSHIP...

What kind of thing do you look for in a good friend?
"People who are funny as well as understanding."

How important are good friends to you?
"So important! My friends mean so much to me. If I have a problem I can call them, or if I'm sad they'll cheer me up. It's nice to have people who understand you and know stuff about you. I have a close group of friends."

Is it hard to make genuine friends in Hollywood?
"Definitely. I think it's hard everywhere when you're an actress. In LA people have a persona and an attitude. I've grown up there so I've had my group of friends for a while. I don't make that many new ones."

In *Wild Child*, one of your friends is a back-stabber, have you ever had a frenemy like that?

"I think everyone deals with frenemies, I've definitely met people who are really nice to your face but talk bad about you. That's so lame."

What would you do if a friend stole your boyfriend?

"I probably wouldn't talk to either of them ever again. It's not one of those things that just happens, they obviously have to go behind your back and get together. That's not cool."

BFFS

THEY MAY BE BEST BUDS, BUT HOW MUCH DO ASH AND NESS REALLY HAVE IN COMMON? WE COMPARE A FEW OF THEIR FAVORITE THINGS...

What	Ashley Vs	Vanessa
Snack	Chocolate, *Gummi Bears*	Peanut butter, crackers
Movie	*Peter Pan*	*Moulin Rouge*
Animal	*Penguin*	*Cheetah*
Color	Pink	Red
School subject	English	Science
HSM song	*Breaking Free*	*Sneaker Night*
Sport	Basketball	Shopping
Hot celeb	Shia LaBeouf	Zac Efron

Ultra Clutch
HAIRSPRAY
PROFESSIONAL
OF THE MOVIE
SHAPER PLUS
NEW LINE CINEMA
A TimeWarner Company
PROFESSIONAL

LITTLE MISS POSITIVE

PERK UP AND STAY POSITIVE WITH THESE CELEB-GALS WORDS OF WISDOM...

BE TRUE TO YOU...

Kelly Osbourne: *"People tell you you're going the wrong way, when it's simply a way of your own..."*

Don't let other people get you down, just focus on being yourself—it hasn't done Kelly Osbourne any harm! Who cares if everyone else does things differently? It's the original, individual types who stand out from the crowd. Look at Gwen Stefani too—she and Kelly have both rocked some unconventional styles in their time. Now their quirks are a huge part of the reason they're considered fabulous. As long as you're happy, who cares what others think?

LAUGH IT OFF...

Vanessa Hudgens: *"You get upset for a little while—'cause you're human. Then you laugh it off and let it go."*

Your BFF embarrasses you in front of your crush, so how do you react? Well, you could yell at her, lose her as a friend and worry you've got no chance with him now. Or you could make like Vanessa Hudgens—laugh it off and forget about it. Some things aren't worth getting upset about, so try putting them into perspective. The smaller the deal you make about it, the sooner it'll be forgotten. This will leave a less stressed, more positive you!

FEEL GOOD INSIDE...

Taylor Swift: *"Every girl has days when she doesn't like her appearance, but it's when you feel happy in yourself that you look good."*

You can buy a dress, slap on the make-up and wear new shoes, but as singing superstar, Taylor Swift says, if you find yourself feeling down, get up and get moving! Eat well, sleep well and exercise—even if it's just a power walk to the mall. A healthy you, is a happy you—you'll feel more motivated in no time!

GIRLS ROCK!

GIRLOLOGY

GIRLOLOGY

ARE YOU MAD ABOUT MILEY?

1. What is the name of Miley's dad in *Hannah Montana*?

A. Stewart Robinson

B. Robbie Stewart

2. Miley Cyrus was born in what state?

A. Tennessee

B. Illinois

3. Her favorite kind of take-out food is...

A. Indian

B. Chinese

4. Which famous singer played Miley's aunt in *Hannah...*?

A. Dolly Parton

B. Celine Dion

5. What is Miley's birth date?

A. October 5, 1991

B. November 22, 1992

Score one point for each correct answer:

★ **0–2 points: Clueless** ★

Girl, you have some serious fact finding to do!

★ **3–5 points: Superfan!** ★

Wow! You know tons about Miley—you're a total fan-girl!

Answers: 1 – B, 2 – A, 3 – B, 4 – A, 5 – B

WHAT'S YOUR PERFECT HAIRSTYLE?

START HERE

Do you love to spend your money on styling products?
NO
YES

If you need a boost, do you get a new 'do or new clothes?
CLOTHES
HAIR DO

Would you ever dye your hair a really bright color?
NO
YES

How long do you spend doing your hair?
UNDER 15 MINS
OVER 15 MINS

Do you have more hair accessories than jewelry?
NO
YES

Rihanna's smooth bob or Amanda Bynes' long, loose curls?
AMANDA
RIHANNA

You usually ask your hair stylist for...

A trim

The full works

What's your styling essential—hairspray or head bands?

Hair bands

Hairspray

Do your friends ever nag to you to leave your hair alone?

NO

ALWAYS

A—*Simple Styling*
Hair stylists? No thanks! Like Amanda Bynes, you prefer to keep your hair *au naturel* and think that styling products are a big waste of money. As for fussy barettes and clips, you just don't get why anyone deals with them!

B—*Top of the Crops*
You like to mix it up—on casual days you'll just tie your hair back, but if it's a special occasion, you'll style it from root to end. You love to experiment and, like Demi, have a hair 'do to be jealous of, not to mention a fabulous collection of accessories.

C—*Fancy Formal*
Your hair is your crowning glory—you love fussing with it and, like Selena, wearing it every which way possible. Be careful though, over use of harsh products can wreak havoc on your tresses. So limit your use of curling irons and always use a protective spray with them.

ARE YOU A CHRISTINA KNOW-IT-ALL?

★★★★★★★★★

TAKE OUR QUIZ TO FIND OUT!

1. What was the name of Christina's debut single?
A. *What a Girl Wants*
B. *Genie In A Bottle*
C. *Come On Over Baby*

2. When is Christina's birthday?
A. December 18, 1980
B. June 18, 1989
C. December 18, 1880

3. What's her cute husband called?
A. Jordan Bartman
B. Jordan Simpson
C. Jordon Bratman

4. Which animated film did she sing *Car Wash* for?
A. *Shark Tale*
B. *Finding Nemo*
C. *Monsters, Inc.*

5. When she was younger, which celeb did she work with on TV show *The Mickey Mouse Club*?
A. Ashlee Simpson
B. Britney Spears
C. Hilary Duff

CHRISTINA AGUILERA

6. What's her middle name?
A. Jane
B. Sarah
C. Maria

Answers: 1B 2A 3C 4A 5B 6C

THE REAL RIHANNA!

HOW MUCH DO YOU REALLY KNOW ABOUT THE MUSIC SUPERSTAR?

1. Rihanna's full name is...
A. Rihanna Robyn Fenty
B. Robyn Rihanna Fenty
C. Rihanna Roberta Fenty

2. Her star sign is...
A. Aries
B. Gemini
C. Pisces

3. She once won a...
A. Beauty pageant
B. Talent show
C. Poetry recital

4. As well as owning a dog called Marley, Rih has a pet...
A. Snake
B. Spider
C. Turtle

5. Rih plays a cameo role in...
A. *High School Musical 3*
B. *Bring It On 3: All or Nothing*
C. *Cruel Intentions 3*

Answers: 1B, 2C, 3A, 4C, 5B

WHICH GOSSIP GIRL ARE YOU?

FIND OUT WHICH SUPER-SOCIALITE COULD BE YOUR TWIN SIS!

If you were dressing to reflect your personality, your outfit would be…

A. Relaxed but cool
B. Cute and girly
C. Sassy n' stylish

Your friends want to go bowling but you'd rather see a movie. You…

A. Try to convince them that a movie's a better idea
B. Just go along with whatever they want
C. Tell them you're all seeing a movie, and that's that

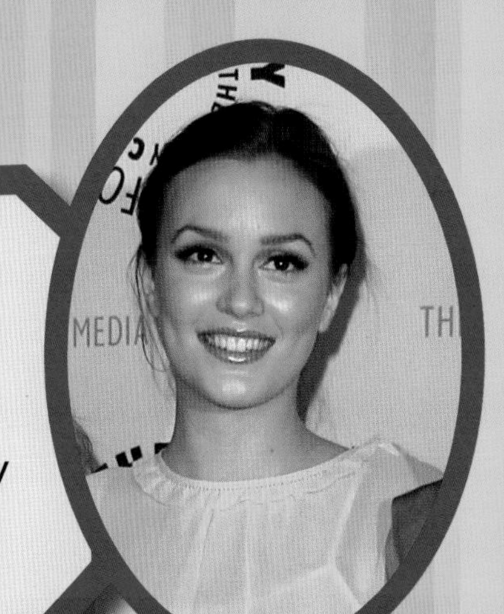

It's Saturday afternoon—where are you?

A. Chilling out in a cozy café
B. At home, spending time with your family
C. Getting ready for a party, of course!

Which of these personality types sound like you?

A. Strong but sensitive
B. Shy
C. A born leader

A friend confides in you, making you swear to absolute secrecy. You...

A. Keep what she's told you to yourself
B. Stay quiet 'til someone asks about it
C. Tell all to the first person who'll listen to you

Mostly As—*Serena*

Just like Ms van der Woodsen, you're at your happiest when you're chilling out with friends, and you try your best to avoid too many formal situations! Your laid-back personality shows through in the way you dress and style yourself. You tend to go for guys who have their feet on the ground and, even though you sometimes get things wrong, you genuinely try to look out for your pals.

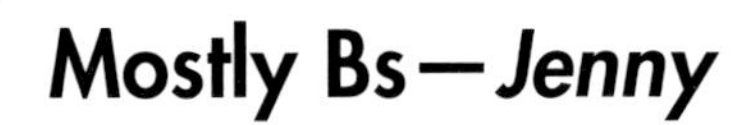

Mostly Bs—*Jenny*

Dan's little sister is a super-sweet girl, just like you. Gal pals constantly ask your advice about their outfits and, despite your shy nature, you're still a hit with the boys! Family is important to you and so are your friends. If there's something you want to do, or place you want to go, then say so—don't miss out!

Mostly Cs—*Blair*

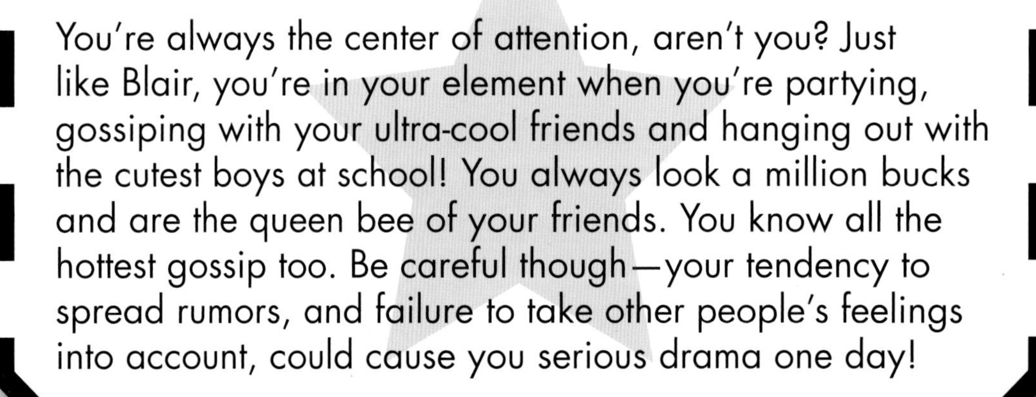

You're always the center of attention, aren't you? Just like Blair, you're in your element when you're partying, gossiping with your ultra-cool friends and hanging out with the cutest boys at school! You always look a million bucks and are the queen bee of your friends. You know all the hottest gossip too. Be careful though—your tendency to spread rumors, and failure to take other people's feelings into account, could cause you serious drama one day!

THE PALEY CENTER FOR MEDIA

WHICH STARLETS COULD YOU ROCK WITH?

START HERE

Do you love everything to do with pop music?

TOTALLY

NO

When you're performing, you prefer to...

SING

DANCE

Do you feel more comfy on your own or in a big group?

Solo—more eyes on me!

Big group of besties

Would you ever enter a talent show?

I'm the next Jennifer Hudson!

No—they're so lame!

The more paparazzi attention, the better?

Oh yeah!

Not necessarily

You'd describe yourself as...

Classy

Sassy

Are you fazed by the thought of a celeb lifestyle?

Hmmm, it could be tough → A

Not a bit ↓

Stage outfits—the showier the better?

Ew... tacky! → A

Bring it on! ↓

Your dreams of success involve you being...

The best → B

An international superstar! → C

A—*Hannah Montana*
All your life you've dreamed of wowing audiences and you'll do anything to make it happen. Your journey to the top may be tough at times but self-belief and talent will get you there.

B—*Rihanna*
Like this streetwise songstress, you're confident, determined and don't suffer fools gladly—that's a big part of your success and cool image. You have the ambition and confidence to back up your abilities, just don't get too arrogant and you'll rock out, big-time!

C—*Pussycat Dolls*
You have a rep for being a show-off—usually among people who are jealous of you! So what if you love the limelight? At least you're happy to share it with your gang. So go make some moves on the stage, girlfriend!

GUESS THE SONG LYRICS!

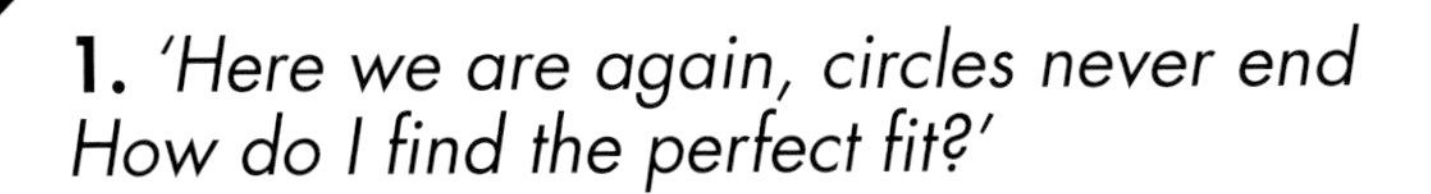

LIKE TO SING-ALONG TO YOUR FAVE SONGS? LET'S SEE HOW EASY YOU FIND THESE TUNE TEASERS!

1. *'Here we are again, circles never end*
How do I find the perfect fit?'

....

2. *'Stick to the stuff you know*
It is better by far
To keep things as they are'

....

3. *'When the war has took its part*
When the world has dealt its cards
If the hand is hard, together
We'll mend your heart'

....

4. *'A thousand miles seems pretty far*
But they've got trains and planes and cars
I'd walk to you if I had no other way'

....

5. *'You're way too beautiful girl*
That's why it'll never work'

....

6. *'I never read your letter 'cause I knew*
what you'd say
Give me that Sunday School answer
Try and make it all OK'

....

Answers:
1. Soulmate, Natasha Bedingfield
2. *Stick to the Status Quo*, High School Musical
3. *Umbrella*, Rihanna
4. *Hey there Delilah*, Plain White T's
5. *Beautiful Girls*, Sean Kingston
6. *Never Again*, Kelly Clarkson

CHICK FLICKS

TEST YOUR KNOWLEDGE OF THESE CLASSIC GIRL MOVIES...

Across

2. Christmas feel-good movie Love________(8)
4. Mean Girl Lindsay______________(5)
6. British diary diva ____________Jones (7)
7. Drew Barrymore comedy, Never Been_________(6)
8. Amanda Bynes' love triangle romantic comedy (11)

Down

5 Channing Tatum's dance debut (4,2)
6. Hilary Duff's A___________Story (10)
4. She's All That cutie, Freddie_____________Jr. (6)

Across:
2. Actually 4. Lohan 6. Bridget 7. Kissed 8. Lovewrecked
Down:
5. Step Up 6. Cinderella 4. Prinze

WHICH SUPERHERO ARE YOU?

WHOSE SASSY SUIT IS LURKING UNDER YOUR CURRENT FASHION ENSEMBLE?

Your friends would probably describe you as...
A. Quiet and shy
B. A bit of a show-off
C. Considerate but confident

If you could choose just one superpower what would it be?
A. Lightning speed
B. The ability to control my surroundings
C. To become invisible

Which kind of superhero outfit would you prefer?
A. Something unusual, edgy and customized
B. A practical but sassy jumpsuit
C. Something sporty that lets me move easily

Would you describe yourself as an easy-going sort of girl?
A. Not really, I play by my own rules
B. Not at all, I'm a control freak
C. Yes, as long as that's okay with everyone else

Mostly As—*Catwoman*

Just like Ness might be as *Catwoman*, you may seem a bit quiet in your everyday life but, when it matters, your strong, confident side emerges. You value your independence and feel that, if you want a job done right, you need to do it yourself!

Mostly Bs—*Storm*

Courageous, cool and a born leader, you're just like the *X-Men* gal...or, in this case, our very own Ms Lively! Your intelligence and determination inspire people, who may feel you have a mystical edge too. Be aware of what's going on and you'll be invincible!

Mostly Cs—*Invisible Woman*

Wow! What a force for good you are! As is Natasha B—like you, she's kind, thoughtful and a great team player. Your powers may not be as in-your-face as traditional superheroes, but like Fantastic Four's Sue Storm, people would be dumb to underestimate you.

WHICH HSM GIRL ARE YOU?

START HERE

What's your favorite type of outfit?
- Dress or a cute top and skirt
- Tee and jeans

How do you spend your Saturday nights?
- Out partying
- On the sofa, watching TV

Studying—fun and challenging or a total pain?
- Pain
- Fun

Do you get involved in any after-school activities?
- Sometimes, not often
- Yes all the time

Are you a mall-girl or a designer diva?
- Designer
- Mall

Books or Magazines?
- Mags
- Books

Do you feel frazzled about leaving your comfort zone?

Yes

No—few things faze me!

Do you love to sing?

Absolutely!

Not really

You've got more of a talent for which subject at school?

Drama

Math

A—*Gabriella*
You're a little on the shy side, but everyone likes you because you're so kind hearted. You have many obvious plus points, like your intelligence, but if you came out of your shell your other talents would surprise people big-time!

GABRIELLA

B—*Sharpay*
You're the 'It' girl of your school, the life and soul of the party who loves to socialize. You're confident, with loads of personality but can be pushy—so be careful not to get in people's faces!

SHARPAY

C—*Taylor*
You're a calm and down-to-earth person. Partying isn't really your thing—you'd much rather chill out with a good book, or maybe watch a TV documentary. You've got a genius brain and always score amazing grades!

TAYLOR

GIRLS ROCK!

STYLE GIRL

STYLE GIRL

WE WANT HER WARDROBE!

Check it out!
It's no secret that bold prints are a great look and Demi totally works them in this awesome checked dress teamed with black tights—cutesville city!

Rockin' the red carpet!
Demi shuns the typical glam-girl, red-carpet look and rocks up in an all-black, skinny jeans and top ensemble—proof that understated cool beats over-the-top frills any day!

Totally unique!

Not afraid to stand out from the crowd, Demi can be a real risk-taker when it comes to stepping out. Here she mix and matches a sparkly beret, a cute bow tie and a gray short jumpsuit—it really shouldn't work, but Demi's got it going on!

Military chic!

Demi knows that a button-up, military-style jacket is the perfect cover-up for any outfit. It looks super-cute with girly, *au naturel* hair and make-up.

BAREFACED CHIC

Paris Hilton

Paris may be wondering where her make-up bag is, but she shouldn't worry, she looks awesome without it!

Anne Hathaway

Anne Hathaway proves that, while *The Devil Wears Prada*, she doesn't need to wear lipstick to look amazing!

Hayden Panettierre

Fresh-faced and friendly, Hayden is always one of our *Heroes* when it comes to looking gorgeous!

Miley

Miley still manages to be super-smiley even without foundation!

Ashley Tisdale

Ashley didn't have time to re-apply her lip gloss before leaving the gym, but that doesn't matter, she's still able to look super-awesome!

Vanessa Hudgens

Au naturel is a term that must have been invented for Vanessa—look how she rocks this no-make-up look!

BEAUTY 101

Lauren Conrad

If your nose is bigger than you'd like, here's a hint to make it look slimmer: blend highlighter down the center and shade with bronzer at the side. Make sure to blend together well so you don't look two-toned.

Avril Lavigne

If you're a pale girl by nature, don't attack yourself with all the fake tan you can get. Tanner isn't always better, especially if it looks super-false. Take a page out of Dita, Avril and Gwen's books: embrace your beautiful complexion and stand out from the crowd!

Leighton Meester

Stand. Up. Straight. We can't say it enough! Good posture makes you look longer and leaner instantly. Use your locker if your backpack weighs a ton. Do you really need all those books right now?

Taylor Swift

Take a tip from Taylor Swift and don't go overboard with the make-up. The key is to look naturally stunning without trying too hard. You'll be revered as a beautylicious babe!

STAR STYLE

CHECK YOUR HOROSCOPE AND GET THE LOOK!

ARIES

You want a look that's easy to achieve, because Aries girls would rather be out there having fun than messing around in front of the mirror!
Get the look: Jeans with a fantastic sequined belt, like Fergie's, give you the casual style that you love, but dresses you up enough for any party. Slick on some lip gloss for extra shine!

Fergie

TAURUS

It's all about comfort. You don't care how cool something looks—if it's a pain to wear it'll stay in your closet.
Get the look: Go for easy-to-wear sports gear, it's perfect for helping you feel really comfy!

GEMINI

You love fashion so it has to be super-stylish, but with an individual twist. Light, bright colors like sky blue and yellow will boost your mood, big time!
Get the look: Invest in some hair gel and have fun coming up with different looks to match your changeable moods!

CANCER

Hippie chic is such a good look on you! It totally suits your arty streak and brings out the real dreamer in you.
Get the look: Shimmery eye shadow brings out the best in your eyes. And you carry off floaty, lacy summer dresses.

Ashley Tisdale

LEO

A Leo lady needs stunning, distinctive clothes that'll stop people in their tracks at 100 paces. If you're going to wear it, it's gotta be something special, so save up for that one show-stopping outfit like Ashley's dress.
Get the look: Strut your stuff in matching accessories!

VIRGO

You'd never be seen in anything that didn't look totally fabulous, dah-ling. And why would you want to be? You *ARE* fabulous!
Get the look: True beauty comes from the inside, so eat a healthy, balanced diet and drink lots of water—then you'll be gorgeous inside and out!

LIBRA

You're a tomboy, but now and again you'll get the urge to be more girly. Shades of blue, rose-pink and light greens are best for you.

Get the look: Polish your toenails pink and stick on flower transfers.

SCORPIO

Anything you wear looks good on you—and no one would ever tell you otherwise! Black and dark red fit your dramatic personality.

Get the look: Wear dark, glossy nail polish for some midnight magic!

Mischa Barton

SAGITTARIUS

You like the casual look, but when you put on the glitz... wow! Your gal pals love your fashion tips, too!

Get the look: If it sparkles, it's got your name on it! You love pink and accessorize to the max!

★ CAPRICORN ★

You're obsessed with the detail and love nothing more than workin' it in a stylish, practical outfit. But you hate it when your clothes don't match.

Get the look: You're amazing at making things, so why not grab a jewelry kit and make some cute accessories?

Natasha Bedingfield

★ AQUARIUS ★

Like Mischa Barton you've got your own style—wacky, individual and trendsetting. You spend hours searching out one-of-a-kinds, so there's no way anyone can steal your look.

Get the look: Grab a top with an unusual print and finish off with shimmery lip gloss and a jeweled fake tattoo.

★ PISCES ★

Keep cool in mermaid colors like aquamarine, deep blue and green. You love dressing up and never hold back.

Get the look: Your soul sister eyes are your best feature. Wear lilac and amethyst to show them off.

STYLE GIRL

DRESSED TO IMPRESS

GWEN'S OUR FAVE POP AND FASHION ICON AND ALL-ROUND QUIRKY CHICK—NO DOUBT ABOUT IT!

She is a fashion designer!

"I have a whole range of fashion merchandise called L.A.M.B. which stands for Love Angel Music Baby. Plus there's another, called Harajuku Lovers, inspired by Japanese street style."

She's always had star style!

"When I was in school, they'd ask: 'what are you going to be when you grow up?' And then you'd have to draw a picture of it. I drew myself dressed in a totally crazy outfit with a microphone—not too far off was I?!"

She loves shoes!

"Sometimes you have to sacrifice your stage performance for high heels."

She adores playing dress up

"Being in music, you can wear whatever you want—it's like an excuse for Halloween every day!"

She's a style icon!

"I think I've been able to fool a lot of people into thinking I'm pretty hip, but in reality I'm just a dork!"

STYLE GIRL

POSH POUT!

FOLLOW THESE HOT HINTS TO GET A STAND-OUT POUT JUST LIKE YOUR FAVE CELEBS!

GET LIPPY!

Don't ever use a tester lipstick on your mouth—it's super-unhygienic and icky! If you can't tell whether the shade's suitable just by looking, test the color on your fingertips. They're a closer match to your lips than the back of your hand.

The most important rule is don't overload your face with color. If your lips are bold, keep your eyes subtle. If you're going for dramatic eyes, apply a transparent shine to your pout!

If you like the natural look but wanna amp it up, choose a lipstick two shades darker than your normal color.

Got a lipstick that isn't really you? Use a lip brush to blend it with other colors 'til you get the shade that suits you better.

Rihanna goes back to the 80s with matt-finish lipstick in a funky neon pink shade.

Kelly O's glam-girl pout is all about the Hollywood glamour. Paint your lips with a bright red lipstick and add a slick of gloss over the top for full impact!

Christina's old-school Hollywood glam looks just right with her glossy red lips and blonde hair.

STYLE GIRL

STYLIN' WITH
SELENA!

SUPER-GENEROUS SELENA GOMEZ SHARES HER TIPS ON HOW TO STEAL HER LOOK...

Shop Around
"I especially love to look around thrift stores for really cool, funky shirts."

Cool n' casual
"I don't really like dressing up. Some people think actresses dress up everywhere they go. I'm in sweatpants half the time with my hair in a ponytail."

Customize
"My style's actually pretty cheap—anyone can have it. It's more about putting a little of you into it."

Comfort is Key
"I can't dress in something that I'm not comfortable in. I can't do dresses or extreme high heels."

Adapt and Accessorize
"I find my own way of dressing up. I like to add cool bracelets or skinny jeans. I try to find a happy medium."

GIRLS ROCK!

GIRL
TALK

KEIRA KNIGHTLEY

SHE'S GORGEOUS, TALENTED AND GLOBALLY FAMOUS....SHE'S KEIRA KNIGHTLEY!

KEIRA ON...

Being a style icon
"The girl in me goes, 'ooh, that's exciting!' But I don't think you can take it too seriously!"

Seeing herself on the big screen
"It's weird! I just don't think it's very good most of the time, so I just watch the wheels turn and think, 'oh, why did you do it like that?'

Auditions
"My most embarassing audition was for The Phantom of the Opera, as I knew I couldn't sing the part! Operatically trained Emmy Rossum bagged it instead!"

Feeling insecure
"I think people have to be happy in their own bodies and, as long as you are, that's great."

PSSSt!

At the age of 20, Keira was the third youngest woman in Oscar history to be nominated for Best Actress, for Pride and Prejudice.

PSSSt!

A dress of hers was auctioned, raising a whopping $8,600 for the British charity Oxfam.

PSSSt!

Her first name means 'Dark'.

CUTE!

RIHANNA RULES!

FROM BAGGING A BOY TO SHARING STYLE TIPS, THE SINGER SPILLS THE BEANS...

Be a Boy Magnet

"When I like a boy, I always start by hanging out with him as part of a group. That way, it's easier to flirt with him as there's no one-on-one pressure. Most of my boyfriends have started out as friends first."

Charitable Chick

"When I was younger, I'd watch television and see all the children around the world suffering. So, I always said to myself, 'when I grow up I want to help.'"

Big-screen Dreams

"Movies and acting is another thing that I want to get into. I think it's really cool but I want it to be right. I don't want it to be forced or to do anything that'll give me a bad acting reputation, but I'm going to be getting into that very soon."

Foxy Fashionista

"I'm tired of not finding clothes I love, so I'm designing my own range. I'm very hands-on with it, just to make sure it's cutting-edge and that it really speaks for who I am!"

DOWN TO EARTH DATERS

AS A-LISTERS, THEY'VE GOT THEIR PICK OF THE PREMIERES AND RED-CARPET PARTIES TO GO TO. BUT THESE COOL CELEBS ALL PREFER TO KEEP IT REAL...

ASHLEY TISDALE

"Because I'm never at home, I think it's ok to do a movie marathon with pizza. Or we'll walk my dog, Blondie, on the beach. When you like someone, it doesn't matter what you do if you're together."

AVRIL LAVIGNE

"I'm into spontaneous things—it doesn't have to be mapped out, like, 'oh, we're going to do dinner from 5pm to 7pm'. I'd rather be with someone who is going to be, like, 'let's go scare ourselves at a haunted house!', or 'let's go surfing!'"

MISCHA BARTON

"I hate formal dates. My ideal date would probably be a concert, where there's good music and we can talk and hang out. But I think my best dates have been walking around, going into stores, going to the park... and then it turns into a night out because you're having so much fun together."

TAYLOR SWIFT

"I love really romantic gestures, but as I'm always so busy the perfect date for me would just be to hang out, kick-back and watch a really good romantic movie!"

FACE VALUE

WHAT DO THEIR FACIAL FEATURES REALLY SAY ABOUT OUR FAVE CELEBS? WE'VE DONE SOME SPECIAL FACE-READING (PHYSIOGNOMY) TO FIND OUT...

PARIS

Paris's pointed nose tells us she's a romantic kind of girl. She loves to be swept off her feet and treated like a total princess. Her low-set eyebrows also hint that she's smarter than her public image might suggest. Behind the blonde party girl is a very savvy empire builder.

VANESSA

Vanessa's pointy chin indicates her fun, flirty nature. She's always up for a laugh, which is why she's so incredible in the *High School Musical* movies. At the same time, her lips tell us she's a realist, especially when it comes to relationships. No wonder she fell for a boy who understands the demands of a showbiz career.

HAYDEN

Hayd's narrow eyes betray her secretive side. Despite being a huge star, she likes to keep her personal life private, especially her relationship with *Heroes* co-star Milo Ventimiglia. Her large forehead corresponds to her sensitive nature, explaining why she's such a committed cheerleader in real life.

CRUSHABLE GUYS

BEING A GIRL ROCKS BECAUSE WE GET TO CRUSH ON THESE GUYS—OMG!

TOTAL HOTTIE

Seriously, what's not to love about **Zac?**

When he smiles, **Corbin** is totally cute!

TOTAL HOTTIE

The **Jo Bros** are three crushes in one cute boy band package!

TOTAL HOTTIE

TOTAL HOTTIE
Crushing on **Chace** is the perfect way to use your time!
TOTAL HOTTIE
Penn works the 'mean and moody' look so well!
TOTAL HOTTIE
Ne-Yo's smile could melt your heart at 100 paces. Sigh.

CELEB CRINGE!

IT'S NOT JUST US REGULAR GIRLS WHO HAVE JAW-DROPPING EMBARASSING MOMENTS!

MILEY CYRUS

"It's really embarrassing when you forget the words to your own song! The other day, I forgot the words to See You Again, and that song plays 24/7. How I forgot the words I don't know!"

VANESSA HUDGENS

"When we were shooting HSM2, Zac spins me around in a song called Every Day. It was windy and my dress blew up, so everyone saw my underwear!"

LEIGHTON MEESTER

"On set one day, I just got complete memory block and I forgot my lines. Not just once but for the whole day. I was calling characters the wrong name and my words were all coming out wrong!"

TAYLOR SWIFT

"I tripped over my microphone on stage and my skirt blew up at the same time—I was so embarrassed! I just kept singing and hoped that no one noticed!"

ASHLEY TISDALE

"At school, I tripped over a fire extinguisher in front of the whole football team!"

ALL ABOUT AMANDA

AMANDA BYNES, STAR OF HAIRSPRAY AND ROBOTS, TELLS US HOW TO MAKE IT BIG IN THE MOVIES...

You started acting when you were 10. Was it hard to cope?
"Yeah. From the age of 13 to 16 it was hard, 'cause I was going between school and The Amanda Show [her own sketch series, which featured Drake & Josh and Adam Brody] which was hard. I felt left out of things that happened with friends when I wasn't there. As soon as I'd get into it all again, I'd have to go back to the show."

It must have been cool starring in your own show though?
"It was very cool. I was in every scene, so it was exhausting but it was lots of fun."

What's a secret about the movies?
"That we're not Perfect Skin, Nice Hair robots—no one has perfect skin or good hair ALL the time!"

What are your acting tips?
"First, watch movies—it's a good way to learn. Take acting classes if you can and always practice—do anything to challenge yourself. And ask your parents for support 'cause you'll need it!"

 PSSSt! 

Amanda starred in a Bruncha Crunch candy TV ad when she was just seven!

HILARY ON HILARY

LOVED HER AS LIZZIE MCGUIRE? LOVE HER ROCKIN' HER STUFF ON STAGE? HILARY DUFF HAS BEEN THERE AND DONE THAT...AND SO MUCH MORE! FOLLOW HILZ THROUGH HER CRAZY CAREER SO FAR...

The movie *Casper Meets Wendy*
"This was my first major role and I was so green. I didn't really know what I was doing. I just did what the director told me to do!"

Lizzie McGuire
"This was such a crazy time for me because I became famous overnight. I went from an unknown Texas girl to not being able to go to the mall without being mobbed by kids! I loved being Lizzie!"

Her debut CD, *Metamorphosis*
"I was so young when I released this; I've changed so much since then!"

The Movie, *A Cinderella Story*
"Every girl's dream is to be Cinderella and I got to live it in this movie. Aren't I lucky?"

***With Love...Hilary Duff*—the perfume**
"I had so much fun developing my fragrance. I was able to go into the lab and work with the perfumer on selecting notes until we got it just right."

Six year old Hilary starred with her older sis Haylie in the ballet, The Nutcracker Suite!

CUTE!

LOOKING HOT